I0164329

Songs Without Music

And Other Poems

Rev. David E. Clarke

Rev. David E. Clarke

The Bible used in this book is from the NKJV.
This book was printed in the United States of America.
To order additional copies of this book, contact:

Rev. David E. Clarke
P.O. 82
Ashville, Ohio 43103

Published by FWB Publications
Columbus, Ohio

This book is dedicated in loving memory
to Mom and Dad
to my family
to my church
to Timothy and Dr. Jim
to Ernie and Mae
and foremost to my Lord:

Ho Kurios Mou Kai Ho Theos Mou

A DIFFERENT PATH

The light
The might
I moved from the main
Creating a strain
The Lord my preeminent sight

They push for more
From their store
They say do the norm
Avoid the storm
But I have a different chore

To amass like they
To do what they say
Do not think old
But grab the gold
Listen to their modern bray

I reach for Him
Forget their whim
Turn back the clock
Anchor to His dock
The material will only dim

They travel too far down their road
Allowing a selfish goad
Ignoring the right
Becoming a fallen knight
Absorbing a selfish load

Not for me
Only He can I see
He is my Lord
I speak His sword
It is all I can be

I have turned my back
I considered their aim, their lack
I have counted the cost
I choose not to be lost
But there comes their attack

I walk the old way
Against their modern sway
I look to His path
I am relieved from His wrath
Coming in His day

They rush to the fore
Coveting the more
They want
The material is their flaunt
Rushing past me to an opposite shore

I push back
From an inevitable attack
So many of them
My number so slim
My number so slack

They say we are right
Look at our might
You are few
We must be true
You are a blight

I stand
I can
He is
Nothing amiss
I must be a man

He is true
Though the number is few
His way will grow
To those who wish to know
His way is due

The numbers belie
The common thought makes you die
Apart from Him
Covered with sin
I cannot be their ally

I must stand
I will, I can
Suffering their barb
Suffering their harm
I see the eternal land

On and on
They say you must belong
Not to old ways
Not like in now gone days
Only in the 'me' can you be strong

Of course they lie
They see the short and then they die
They cast away and far
The eternal divine star
To Him I'll draw nigh

I am bonded and sure
In Him I am secure
Thought by them to be a fool
But I cannot be their tool
I will avoid and ignore their lure

Soon the day will loom
As the bride I will see the Groom
He will call me from this land
And on distant glory I will stand
Choosing life lieu the doom

Immersed in His love as a bath
I will not see the wrath
Of those who chose the wrong
Whose greed rose so strong
I chose a differing path   7-28-2015

COME SWEET ANGELS

O sweet angels take his hand,
      lead him to the promised land
He knew such pain while He was here,
      give him peace and remove the tear

Come sweet angels help my friend
Come for his time in glory begins
Come sweet angels, come today
Come and carry my brother away

O sweet angels help him along
      for he brought joy and he was strong
He gave help to all of us,
      take him now to Lord Jesus

O sweet angels hear my plea,
      guide my brother to Christ's knee
For he is safe, in scarred hands,
      cherish my brother, cherish this man.   10-1996

MY LIFE

My life
Such strife
Reaching for Him
Forgiven of my sin
A land, an eternity
A love just for me
His love
The Dove
His grace
In my place
His scarred hand
Reaches for this man
My life is Him
Forgiven of my sin
He is my all
He is my call.

7-29-2015

EVEN ME

I've no tortured cry
     or any weak sigh
I have His strength
     as my quenching drink
If I'm hurt or afraid,
     His blessings He gave.
His face I want to see.
     I know He loves me

My walk is now sure.
     He is my only cure.
When I'm hungry He sustains.
     By His blood I obtain
Some soon glorious day
     This mortal pot of clay,
Will sit my His knee.
     I know He loves me

Even me, even me I know He loves me
He hung there on that tree
Even me, even me I know He loves me
He proved it on Calvary

I'll live in His place
     Through His saving grace.
I'll walk through that gate
     With His clean slate
I'll praise the King of kings
     When the glory-bell rings.
Now He allows me to be,
     I know He loves me   6-1995

PEOPLE

When People don't have much to say,
      they usually say it loudly and with interruption

WITH NO REGRETS

With no regrets, I walk my way
I serve my Lord in my trek
In His house, I will always stay
I walk, I serve with no regrets
Now, time drifts away
The past more than the now
I'll love; I'll work in my remaining days
Soon I'll fly away with no regrets

I loved and I cried
I lived and I tried
I helped, at times I had loss
I worked and I stayed
I sang and I prayed
With no regrets I carried His cross

With No regrets, my race will be run
I'll feel the earth slip away
I'll feel no harm for there's God's Son
When finished, I'll not wish to stay
With no regrets, mortal life is o'er
The task and the strife are done
I'm going to where time is no more
My eternity with the Son

With no regrets, my eternity with my Lord.   5-28-2001

I AM OLD

I am old. I know this fact true and well. Every morning I hear the symphony of groans and bones as I rise from my bed. I prove the second law when I look in the mirror during the night times hours. Regardless of the advertisements, I will not be young and spry again. I am old. Given this reality I now know I know less than I did in my youth. I know there is a God and I know I am not Him. I know this fact both true and absolute.

I PRAISE YOU LORD

I praise you Lord, I praise you Lord
Forever let me be before your face

You my Lord are the one
You my Lord are Lord of all
You my Lord are the Son
Let me hear your holy call

I praise you Lord, I praise you Lord
Forever let me rest in your grace

You my Lord are the one
You my Lord are Lord of all
You my Lord are the Son
Let me hear your holy call

4-18-01

NOW IS THE TIME

Now is the time to lift our voice
Now is the time for our praise
Now is the time, the Lord is near
Let us praise Him all our days.

6-12-2001

MY GOD #1

My God is worthy of my praise
      let me praise Him in all that I am
My God who created the world
      my God who made, my God who can
My God who made provision for me
      and through the cross let me be saved

5-27-1994

O VICTORY, THE VICTORY

O victory, the victory
His victory given to me
O victory, the victory
By the man who walked the sea

Sweet victory, glorious victory
Of the Son from on high
Sweet victory, glorious victory
I'll meet Him in the sky

Forever by His victory
Can my story unfold
Through majesty's love
He gave me blessings untold

I am always unworthy
He still chose me
And in my worthless stead
He bore Calvary's tree

O victory, His victory
My life now begins
Then victory, forever victory
His victory over Adam's sin.

3-1994

ANOINT ME

Anoint this low mortal man
  with your immortal presence
Allow me to the more stand
  in life's arena proving tense

For I am but dirt and clay
  but you, Lord can mold me
Allow me to serve you every day
  I am blind, permit me to see
Cover me with the Spirit's oil
  clothe me in righteous garb
Let me complete your toil
  as I face evil's harm.   3-1995

LOVE #5

Love me lady, read my mind
  To me right words never come
Move to me for I'm locked in place
  Love for me like to rest, the some
Take my hand, I will not pull away
  I cannot reach out, my worth is nil
Come to me and take my heart
  No, you moved away, but I love still. 7-1993

LET ME PRAISE YOUR NAME

Let me praise your name
Let me praise your name
I come my Lord
Let me praise your name
For the winds and sky
       For all creation and even I
See your marvelous love
       Let me praise your name

Let me praise your name
Let me praise your name
I come my Lord
Let me praise your name
In health or when ill
       Let me do your will
For you are my Lord
       Let me praise your name

Let me praise your name
Let me praise your name
I come my Lord
Let me praise your name
You gave all for me
       You allow me to see
For you are my Lord
       Let me praise your name   4-23-2001

A STAR TO A CROSS

A star, the sign of His birth
The cross, the salvation of earth
From a star to a rugged cross
A redeeming path for all once lost
A journey by Him, human and divine
A sojourn that stands the test of time
The star wasn't the brightest light to see
It was the cross bringing God's light to me
Without the Lord I would suffer loss
The plan completed a star to a cross.

3-1995

ADAM'S SIN TO ME

Take from me
Take from my heart
Take from me
Adam's sin curse
You are the one
The only one who could
Take it from me
Lord of the universe
Replace within me
The old man nature
With another which shows
Your grace renown
Help me to stand
To grow dear Sir
To be a worthy jewel
In your holy crown.

2-1992

I CAN BUT LOOK

When life's cares weigh me down
      And there isn't any safe ground
My body and soul are so weak
      There is only one I can seek

I can but look, look to His grace
I can but search, search for His face
I can but touch, touch for His garb
I can but rest He'll keep me from harm
Though I only struggle along
      I prove never ever to be strong
I'm no different from others I've met
      I move so slow on this mortal trek

Some glorious day when I see Him
      And my failures leave with my sin
Till that day I'll cling to His hand
      My Lord will help me to stand

7-1995

BY HIS PASSION

By His passion, I am free
     By His mercy, I now see
Through His gift, I'm made just
     When grave door opens this I'll trust
Because He is righteousness, I'm righteous too
     By His grace, He will see me through
In His Father's presence, I'm set apart
     His given gift, I have a new heart.

        12-1991

ONE MOST LOW

I was lost and burdened down
He removed His divine crown
He helped this sinner here below
His Father's grace to bestow
His precious gift He gave
One most low could be saved
Then and now and forever more
One most low will call Him Lord

One most low, one most low
By His grace He, I now know
He gave the Father His gloried due
Changing me through and through
One most low, one most low
Through my walk He, I will show
A new life I can begin
For my Lord forgave my sin.

        11-1993

I WHO HAD NOTHING

I who had nothing, no nothing to offer Him
      I who had nothing, no nothing but my sin
I who had nothing, nothing to give a King
      Yet He for me salvation did bring

Glory, glory, glory to His name
      Glory, glory, glory to His name
I who had nothing will never be the same
      I who had nothing will praise His holy name

                    3-1996

LIFE'S GREAT FOOL

Life's great fool am I
I didn't even try
Too late on my start
I had a vain sinful heart
Salvation was granted
But sorrows I lamented
For Him my task and goal
To serve with heart and soul
I was a fool for so long
Lord lead and guide me on
In your care all I will place
Let me only show your grace

          6-1992

MY GOD #2

My God who empowers me with His Spirit
    and enables me to tell of Him to all
My God who gives me grace in evil times
    my God who fortifies me to stand tall
My God who will crush evil away
    my God who will see His plan through
My God so worthy of my praise
    let me always praise Him in all I do.

                                                5-27-1994

THE WATERS

The waters are troubled for you
The waters are troubled for you
No time to wait, do not hesitate
The waters are troubled for you

Come and find relief
Come for any need
Come and find relief
Come and hear His plead

The waters are troubled for you
The waters are troubled for you
No time to wait, do not hesitate
The waters are troubled for you

Come and find ease
Come for He is here
Come and find peace
Come He'll dry your tear   4-30-2001

LET ME LOVE THE HURT AWAY

Since I met you even before we spoke or knew
There was within me a final love so real and true
Life to me has been hard; you have walked that way
You are strong and stand, but let me love the hurt away
In these middle years we have been hurt in hurt's sway
I wish a mortal's wish; please let me love the hurt away.

3-1995

HELP ME, USE ME

Come to me Lord, carry me high
Wipe the tear from my eye
In my mortality, I bow and bend
Carry me away, help me my Friend
I am weak and no good to anyone
Especially to you, God's gift and Son
I flitter and waver and fly all around
An unworthy servant, never very sound
In valleys of life, so bleak and dark
You saved me from sin so stark
Your grace, love and word to impart
You mold and perfect my heart
Let me stand and let me walk
To all people of You, let me talk.

2-1992

DAD'S BENDED KNEES

I recall when I was young
  like a minute past I see
I would rise up in the morn
  Dad was on bended knees

On bended knees Dad found his place
On bended knees Dad found grace
On bended knees Dad found reward
On bended knees my Dad found the Lord

Work would come and then was done
  time for bed it would be
On my way to comfort's rest
  Dad was on bended knees

I would think how tall he was
  standing straight like a tree
No one was ever so tall
  as Dad on bended knees

The preacher man would call them around
  to follow the Spirit's heed
Dad would help pray the fire down
  when Dad was on bended knees.

                              10-27-1995

I'LL BE A FRIEND

Sometimes the ones I meet here
     give reason for my pain and tear
But when I'm all alone
     I'll go to His throne
My friend's song will fall on my ear

I'll be a friend when others want to leave
I'll be a friend when others aren't it seems
When others want to hurt
And others are so curt
I'll be a friend said Jesus to me

Sometimes my life seems so wrong
     in travail, I'm not very strong
But when I'm not my best
     His friendship He'll attest
My friend will sing to me His song

Some day when I'm at my less
     and death's door opens the final test
I'll see His open arms
     He'll keep me from all harm
My friend will say come on up and rest.   12-21-1996

LOVE #10

If kindness be a face
      I gaze upon it in you
If sweetness be a hand
      I touch it when I touch you
If love
      If tenderness
            If passion
                  If charm
If all these are, they embody you
      you remain away, an unclaimed reward
My unworth makes me be silent
      striking hard love's fateful chord
I cherish from a distant desire
      for my life and past demand so
But in loving you, I'll never tire
      my love only continues to grow.

                            7-1993

HE FOR ME

I woke from a sleep of fear
I found a day of woe and tear
I'm in want in things I try
But He for me was willing to die
He was God's own willing Son
He proved to all He was the One
No one ever had less than I
But for me, He was willing to die
I'm amazed if only I was solely lost
My Lord would still go to that cross
He who made the blue, blue sky
Save me and was willing to die.   3-1996

LIFE'S STORM

I may be tossed like a leaf
      In a mighty wind's blow
I may find no relief
      any place I go
But in the sway of the storm
      I'll stand from now till then
I'll rest in my lord
      Until someday I'll see Him

In the mid of life's storm
I'll hold to my Lord
I'll find my rest in Him
In the mid of life's storm

My prizes, my gold
      were soon completely gone
Rusty things I tried to hold
      and my life was so, so wrong
But whether with or without
      I'll stand from now till then
And give a victory shout
      when I finally see Him

5-1997

SWEET DOVE

Glory to Your name
Praise to You above all
Glory for Your cross
A wonderful gift of love
None must suffer loss
Glory to You Sweet Dove   8-25-2001

HELP ME #1

Help me shine in this desperate hour
       times when your help I will need
Help me demonstrate your total power
       rough times, help me Lord I plead.   6-1992

MY TORTURED TEARS

Don't fret over my tortured tears
       they wash my soul's pain away
I need my Lord's grace to ease my fears
       only a few know for this I pray
Life seems a most difficult travail
       I walk this peculiar separate way
I need my Lord's peace that never fails
       only a few know for this I pray
Don't fret over my tortured tears
       they cleanse me in so many ways
They purge and make life more clear
       only a few know for this I pray.   7-1993

IF I WERE THE LAST ONE

I was lost in a hole with no end
      I was down with the weight of sin
With nothing good, inside falling me
      my Lord came to save and relieve

If I were the last one before the rapture day
If I were the last one to take the time to pray
If I were the last one to seek Him stead of loss
If I were the last one He'd still go to that cross

Why would a king choose to come
      not just a King, but God's own Son
To purchase and heal someone like me
      to prepare me a place in eternity

I could not ask Him to take my place
      He was the moment of God's loving grace
Then a sinner without good works to give
      through His great love I started to live

It amazes me that a lonely broken man
      could approach and before this King stand
He grabbed my hand while I was in the hole
      He pulled me out and saved my soul.

3-1996

I CAN BUT LOOK

When life's cares weigh me down
     and there isn't any safe ground
My body and soul are so weak
     there is only one I can seek

I can but look, look to His grace
I can but search, search for His face
I can but touch, touch for His garb
I can but rest He'll keep me from harm

Though I only struggle along
     and I am never ever strong
I'm no different from others I've met
     I move so slow on my mortal trek

Some glorious day when I see him
     and my failures leave with my sin
Till that day I'll cling to His hand
     for my Lord will help me stand.

7-1995

LOVE #13

I find the sun in your smile
Dark night finds you away from me
You have my mind and heart
I feel empty when you I don't see
I went from mistake to mishap
Times ago before I met you
I saw what is with what happened along
I now understand what is true
From your eyes, I see your tears
Some from joy, some from life
I just want to be around
I don't want to increase your strife
I find in you my brightest sun
Greenest valleys, bluest skies
You cause my heart to beat
You give me reason to try   3-30-1995

MY GOMER LAND

Gomer, my present mortal time
Selling yourself, dear land of mine
Leaving God's reason and rhyme
Selling yourself for man's bottom line
Warnings and visions given to you
You ignore and greedily you sow
God you no longer let guide you
Sow the wind, a whirlwind God will bestow
Please turn back and turn to Him
Blessings He will give to your place
He will eradicate your selfish sin
He will cover you with His saving grace.   5-28-1994

ONE MOST LOW[1]

When I was one most low
      I became the seed well sown
He gave me so much more
      when He walked through my door

One most low, one most low
Only Him I will show
A new life I'll begin
My Lord forgave my sin
One most low, one most low
Only Him I will show
For the glory is to Him
For my Lord forgave my sin

When I was lost and down
      He removed His royal crown
For a sinner here below
      He brought grace to bestow

Through a gift He did give
      one mow lost can start to live
Then and now and forever more
      one most low will call Him Lord.   6-1995

---

[1] Based on my poem, One Most Low, "Eclectic Essays." FWB Publishing c. 2011.

WHEN NO ONE CARES

All you get is more insults
  Christ helps you stand tall
No one cares and they see your faults
  Christ sends His peace that passes all
All you feel is tempest and strife
  Christ proves He is there
It seems you fail in this hard life
  Christ aids in overcoming the snare
He came to love you
  To die for you
  To rise again for you
  To receive you unto Himself
  Christ will always care.

        12-1991

I CRIED COME TO ME DEAR LORD

I walk so weakly through any trial
  You will help me run the last mile
One day I answered Your heed
  You came to me and filled my need
I cried come to me dear lord
  on Your cause I wish to board
Help me stand and glorify Your name
  I know for me you came
All my unworth and You still loved me
  You carried a cross, walked the sea
My future so brightly does loom
  You rose from a borrowed tomb

        7-1995

MEMORIES OF THAT DAY

When past memories come to me
       Of the way it used to be
When darkness seemed to loom
       And I lived in failure's room
With no meaning in my life
       Filled with violence and strife
Then memories of that day
       When He took my sins away

Memories of that day when He took my sins away
Giving life to me and allowing me to be
He showed me the way, showed me His glorious way
Memories of that day when He helped me to pray

Yes I do remember the time
       Life had no reason or rhyme
Nothing seemed to be true
       I never had a clue
Then my spirit begin to rise
       I took Him as my Christ
With memories of that day
       When He took my sins away
He showed me how to stay
       With memories of His day
Through the vision of His cross
I had to honor His great cost
To be His feet and hands
       To take His gospel to any land
Always to praise His name
       In that day, for me He came

       6-1995

WHEN SHORTLY

When shortly I stand in front of them
I hope and pray I will glorify Him
It can't be long in these changing times
Soon being a Christian will be a crime
I am a Christian and freely this I will voice
No matter the law or plan, I have no choice.   5-25-1994

WALKING BY YOUR SIDE[2]

I come to you Jesus my soul is open wide
         let me receive your blessing as we walk side by side
You always go before me and lead along the way
         knowing I might stumble you never let me stray

I'm walking by your side, on your love I rely
When I'm weak and alone, you claimed me as your own
You lift me when I'm down, soon you'll give to me a crown
To your cause I've die so I'm walking by your side

You give me all I need, near you I'll always stay
         by feasting on your word, you'll guide me day by day
If I take the wrong path, I'll cry to you for help
         your Spirit comes to me and the problems soon melt

Light your fire inside me, revive me once again
         keep me from failing and giving in to sin
Lord fill my soul daily, keep my heart looking up
         help me to give to all so they can fill their cup 3-9-1996

---

[2] Based on the poem, "Walking By His Side," by Becky Billingsley.

I PRAISE YOU LORD

I praise you Lord, I praise you Lord
Let me be forever before your face

For my Lord you are the one
For my Lord you are Lord of all
For my Lord you are the Son
Let me hear forever your holy call

I praise you Lord, I praise you Lord
Let me be forever in your grace

For my Lord you are the one
For my Lord you are Lord of all
For my Lord you are the Son
Let me hear forever your holy call   4-18-2001

LET ME GIVE

Let me give all, what else could I do
The Lord of all creation is most true
Whether I am sick or well, rich or poor
Let me stay the course of my dear Lord
Let me give in my lack or all I possess
Let me give my witness facing life's test
My home or wealth or being or love
Let me give all that I have to the just Dove
I see Him in the blue sky, the lakes, the hills
I hear Him in the thunder and the still
Let me give all, what else could I do
The Lord of all creation is most true.   4-23-2001

HELP ME #2

Help me work and in that time stand
  adversities assail against all and me
Help me radiate your loving plan
  a path I chose on bended knees.

       6-1992

IN THIS WORLD

Against him at every turn
  hate for his poor soul
Knocked down more and more
  but not so final though
Not understood by any
  whether here or there
Once walking in dark corridors
  finding no peace within
Consumed with fear and anger
  consumed with consuming sin
The pain of that time
  the temporary everyday strife
Transcended by the God-man
  who gave to him precious life
Now he lives for the Lord's place
  not made by mortal hand
Freedom from corruption
  free from the fallen band
Sin now not an issue
  the blood has set him free
A King someday in the air
  this redeemed man will see.

      1-1992

I'VE NO OTHER BUT JESUS

I've no other but Jesus
    to Him I've cried
I've no other but Jesus,
    to His cause I've died
The trials will come
    they will I know
I've no other but Jesus,
    to His cross I'll go
I've no other but Jesus
    no other to share
I've no other but Jesus,
    He really cares
Will you follow
    He's the One
I've no other but Jesus
    God's only Son
I've no other but Jesus
    He rules my place
I've no other but Jesus
    He gives His grace
No more valleys I'll live in
I've no other but Jesus
    He forgave my sin
I've no other but Jesus
    He lifts when I'm down
I've no other but Jesus,
    He is safe ground
In all this world
    He is so true
I've no other but Jesus,
    He'll see me through   11-8-1995

IF I AM AN ISLAND

I am an island in a sea of despair
If a stranger, alien in a different plane
I turn to you Lord and your care
Strengthen me as in my burden I strain   6-1992

THE ONE SO TRUE

I was in a valley most low
I thought no farther I could go
Then I thought of His great cost
To keep me from being lost
I am no more ever my own
This hard valley is not my home
For God so loved even me
His Son died on a cursed tree
I know, not enough do I share
In more ways I should care
My worries that I find here
Body's pain and sorrow's tear
Are but memories soon to fade
My Lord my sins forgave
He paid freedom's price
I see through saved eyes
When I finally breathe my last
And eternity's die with me is cast
I will go to Him above
Protected by His saving love
I will see the angels all around
Once I've left this hard valley ground
Redeemed through and through
By Jesus Christ, the one so true.   9-1995

TIMES

Times are worsening the closer I draw
The gulf more distant now than then
My future is secure when Your cross I saw
And separated me from this world of sin
Good company have been there too
Like they to our God we will be true
Others with rule have their own mother ge
But now and forever to Yahweh, I will pray

5-25-1994

GEORGE, TOM, AND PAT

George, Tom, and Pat pledged their lives and all they had
I have nothing except me and I'll give that and be glad
When that moment comes and I have to make the call
To Yahweh let me and my martyr stand most tall
These trying times within this mortal time and space
Will not remove the supreme Father's eternal grace
I in my the final act let me say, "I forgive you"
But to my faith, freedom and my God I must be true
These testing times are the finish of satan's vain plan
Do what you will, I remain free resting in God's hand.

5-25-1994

VALLEYS OR MOUNTS

I have walked in the valley of distress
        I have climbed the mount of success
In all, I must ask Him to carry me along
        and to Him through His grace I belong
        For not life nor strife:
                not perplexity nor mortality
                not sickness nor being less
                not torture nor failure
Will prevail against me due Him
        He raises me above fallen sin
Though I am a failure, He uses me
        He forgave me and allows me to be
        Through Him:
                        life finds purpose
                        strife finds solace
                        perplexity finds ease
                        mortality finds peace
                        sickness finds comfort
                        less finds import
                        torture finds rest
                        failure finds success
In valleys or mounts I strive for His cross
        no matter the trial for in Him I have no loss
Glory and praise for by Him I will walk on
        Hosanna for through Him I am made strong
                                        4-1994

THAT OLD TREE CROSS

Nothing but the cross will do for me
    For my precious Lord died on that tree
He died a death that was intercessory
    He died a death for you and for me

I will glory in a marvelous thing
I will glory in removing sin's sting
I will glory in His act to save the lost
I will glory in that old tree cross

That cross has no curse, it's taken by him
    He took it away when He paid for my sin
His cross is why to earth He came
He was born and died to remove my shame

To glory in His cross is to honor His name
    my Father sent His Son to take my blame
No other one could or ever would do
    He made a way for me. He made a way for you   5-1995

COME SEE THIS MAN

Come see this man I saw
    was said to all around
He knew who I was
    still He offered safe ground
Come see this man I saw
    isn't He the one
Come see this man I saw
    God's own chosen Son.   3-1996

POETIC FAILURE

Not up to the task
Though my lot is cast
Failed efforts to be
Foolish old man to see
All have left me
Poetic failure left to see.   7-16-2001

FOR HE IS COMING

The clouds will move in start of the coming
        the voices will still, in awe of the Son
The birds will light and stop their calling
        all earth will rest, hard travail is done

For He is coming and perfect will be
The Lord of all, all there will see
For He is coming for His throne
The Lord of all will come with His own

Thunders will cease, birth pangs are o'er
        our fears will end, not like it is now
In His kingdom peace is the norm
        In His kingdom all knees will bow

Trumpets will blare to announce His arrival
        the angels will shout the King is now here
The hosts will sing for He's the lord
        pain will resign along with the tear.
                                5-15-1996

THE CITY OF GOD

Let me grow, let me know
      Let me be, let me see

The city where we'll trod
The city of God
Where we soon will go
Where the Son we'll know
The city is coming
The city of the King
Do you see it coming
Do you see our everything
So holy it is for us
So holy the city of love

Let me come to the Son
      Let me be, let me see.
                 12-10-1998

AT THAT PLACE

Look at the woman at the well
For years in her sin she did dwell
She still received His saving grace
She said yes to His saving place
Even Peter who knew divine Him
Betrayed around the fire in sin
Changed his mind, felt the Son's grace
He lived, worked, served in that place.
                 3-15-1994

REDEEMED AND PURCHASED

I'm redeemed by His blood
  I'm purchased by His love
I long for my Father's home
  there forever I will roam
Just think that in a while
  we will run our last mile
We'll cross o'er to the other side
  in His house we will reside.
        9-1995

HIS LIGHTHOUSE

His lighthouse shines His light
God's holy and divine love
His power and eternal might
Showing His gift from above
He rescued me from sin's sway
And the tumult of my dark life
He gave me the peace of day
And took away evil's strife
I thank Him for His gift
And His reminder to me
All my sin He chose to lift
And gave me His lighthouse to see.
       7-16-2001

JONAH'S PLIGHT

Oh the scene of disobedient Jonah's plight
Who chose to run from the Lord's might
He returned and refound the worker's grace
He went to Nineveh and shared God's grace.   3-15-1994

NO ONE'S BEEN A FRIEND LIKE JESUS

In the dark valley, I find myself today
        I may toss and turn every which way
But no matter the how or the where
        I have but one friend I know does care

No one's been a friend like Jesus
He guides my course, He is my source
No one's been a friend like Jesus
He took my sin, He is my friend

The pain can hurt with no home to go to
        Mortal wants each day I must subdue
No matter the case, no matter the snare
        I have one friend I know does care

Troubles with us will always be
        But Jesus' love is present with me
Storm may come, raging everywhere
        I have one friend I know does care.
                            10-1995

THE COMING BACK

Angelic trumpets someday will sound
The Royal One in majesty will trod
The Mount Olivet Hill will split apart
Then a flowing river from the Son of God
Jerusalem the city He will command
His site, His temple, His eternal throne
An earthly rule starting a thousand years
He is God's definitive chief cornerstone
Chains for the defeated adversary
An abyss for the usurper evil one
The Original will overcome the miscopy
For the Victor is God's own Son
Promises fulfilled as He said He would
Covenants maintained, never a step back
He went, but returned as only He could
Restoring this world from the evil attack
Glory to the Messiah and His Father above
Glory for the promises the Spirit did send
What peace in His perfect divine love
Restoring His footstool with His holy mend.

8-1993

HE MADE ME OVER[3]

Like the lion I now have strength
Through His word, He made me over
Like the eagle I now fly high
Through His lordship, He made me over

I thank you Lord for all of this
Your glorious plan never amiss
Your cross, the debt's been paid
Your precious life gladly laid
And I thank you for making me over
Yes I thank you Lord for making me over
My God made me over

Like a child I now love easily
Through His sacrifice, He made me over
Like a friend I now encourage
For the Father, He made me over
Your life at that point didn't end
Man's sinful lot you did mend
Our future hope you did ensure
Our everything you did cure
And I thank you for making me over
Yes I thank you, Lord for making me over
My God made me over.

Michele Whaley and David E. Clarke, 9-1993

---

[3] Based on the poem, Making Me Over, by David E. Clarke, 12-1991, published in "Eclectic Essays." FWB Publishing. c. 2011

LET ME STAND

Let me stand when life throws me down
Let me stand by your gracious power
Let me stand when all else flitters around
Let me stand in this desperate hour
I am nothing and have nothing to give
I need your help to see me through
If I should die or if I should live
Let me follow your cross and holy You.   6-9-1994

LITTLE CHILDREN

Be still little children don't you cry
          Come rest now in His sweet by and by
You were given up, too young to die
          Be still little children come up high

So be still and rest, eat, and sleep
For all are His own chosen sheep
Life too short and not so kind
Find it there in His own time

Now sleep little children all the night
          Find your peace through His might
He hugs and kisses, don't you see
          If not here, then there you can sleep

Come eat little children have your fill
          Hunger and thirst He will still
Abused and hurt by those so vain
          Come eat little children, have no pain.
                              9-20-1996

NO ONE

I am down and depressed
It's my own fault I guess
I live today in a hole so deep
No whisper of rescue or relief
I feel without, I feel alone
Carrying life like a heavy stone
Who would hear, who would care
No one to help, no one share.

7-21-1994

GOD'S MIRACLE

The most blessed of all miracles
Was when He saved worthless me
No other looms so large
When I was faced with eternity
My pains, my sufferings
My many thorns in the flesh
Pass away to selfish insignificance
When my salvation He did address
That is the point I keep in mind
When I pray, beg, and plead
I've already received my miracle
When I answered His heed
This world may ravage my body
This world may assail my mind
But in my spirit and soul
God's miracle proves an eternal kind.

3-1994

AMIDST THE CLOUDS

Casting off my cares and flying above
Touching His divine and eternal love
No more tears or toils of life
Never to be rolled over by this strife
His promise gift given to me
Very soon amidst the clouds I'll be
Ransom paid ticket due His charge
The Lord of creation keeps me from harm
I am redeemed and new in His sight
I am bought through His saving might
My Lord, my Savior, and my God I will see
Very soon amidst the clouds I'll be.   7-6-2000

I WHO HAD NOTHING

I who had nothing, no nothing to offer Him
I who had nothing, no nothing but my sin
I who had nothing, nothing to give a King
Yet He for me salvation did bring.
                          3-1996

MY SEARCHER FRIEND

My friend Jerry, so true in your task
To discover the words and mind of God
Always standing with an answer to cast
Always following the Father's urging prod

My friend, His truth always your goal
To grab the immortal and throw off this time
To remedy and ensure your soul
Making the Lord your only sole rhyme

My friend, along your way and your path
You have become a dear friend of mine
You have helped and eased my life's wrath
You have been a good friend and very kind

Let me thank you for the time given me
And of your wisdom, peace, and thought
Thank you for the friendship you allowed to be
For your purpose, the help to ease my lot

My friend you reached out for the Lord
No nobler way is there to decide to live
You shared with all His pure, great sword
And to all His love and way to give

That river you have cross and we miss you so
You are there with the Lord and always will be
No pain, no tear for you are healed in your soul
As you sit by our Lord's loving divine knee.

9-14-2000

I CLING ON

There are times when I fail, but I cling on
There are times when life assails, but I cling on
There are times when I'm most low, but I cling on
There are times when I move slow, but I cling on

I cling to my Lord, He is all I should be
I cling to His word and pray His grace covers me
I cling to His cross, He is my only way
I cling to His love every night and every day

In dark valleys I reside, but I cling on
All around seems to have lied, but I cling on
My wants may take hold, but I cling on
All I am is ne'er too bold, but I cling on

Soon I'll see His face, till then I'll cling on
I'll live in His place, till then I'll cling on
These days I should do more, still I'll cling on
For He is my Lord and to Him I'll cling on

                                        10-1995

A REFLECTION

My life must be a reflection of Your grace
        this will cause me to be hated here below
Evil times and more are coming to this place
        let me always have your love to show
Come and reside in useless, worthless me
        strengthen this fallible vessel of clay
Guide me so only You will I always see
        for these things Lord, let me always pray. 6-9-1994

LITTLE CHRISTMAS BABE

Little Christmas babe lying in manger low
Little Christmas babe shining with a glow
> Little one Son of God, little one born divine
> Little one child of love, little one so kind

Little Christmas babe future so hard
Little Christmas babe our everything to guard
> Little one do they know, little one the trek ahead
> Little one of your goal, little one lying on your bed

Little Christmas babe love is your claim
Little Christmas babe glory to your name
> Little one ahead's the test, little one your love to me
> Little one now just rest, little one a little one be

11-1995

EVIL'S WIND

Evil's wind blows so constant
Cover me Lord with Your grace
Evil, the dire cold of my lot
My recourse is to seek Your face
Clothe me Lord with the salvation's robe
Flame my spiritual fire till I burn
Guide me to your harbor of safety
Lord only to you let me turn
Make that wind quiet and blow away
As I travel during this mortal life
Help me Lord for I will always need Thee
Guard me from this cause of strife.

6-1992

I WAS THERE

I was there by the skull's mount
     I found that my sin was no longer
I was there around the cross
     I found my faith became stronger
I was there next to the tomb
     I found His promises brought me high
Someday even higher when I am with Him
     I'll find only to Him can I draw nigh
I was there and here and forever will be
     I know that I know that I know
The Lord someday He, I will see
     and in Him I will continue to grow.   10-1993

THOUGHTS

I have some thoughts
Of your great Passion
You came to die for me
I was so unjust, unfit
You hung on a cross, a tree
You gave grace to all
All who choose Your way
Such thoughts for me.   7-7-2015

NO EARTHLY GOOD

Cares of tomorrow may weigh and rise
     They cause such pain and tears in my eyes
I have to remember my real neighborhood
     I'm so full of heaven I'm no earthly good

I'm no earthly good as others may say
I live for the forever not the day to day
I see His cross, not my mortal care
My hope is Him, the one hope I will share

Pain and hurt seems always to be
     This place is no longer home to me
I look to the sky and brush away the tear
     I'm so full of heaven my home is not here

Someday I'll stand in His glorious day
     In that one thought I will always stay
My goals aren't what others think they should
     I'm so full of heaven I'm no earthly good   8-1995

BY MY SAVIOR'S SIDE

When I'm lost with nowhere to go
    I'll cry out to one I know
    I'll find my home by my Savior's side
Sudden night's all around me
    Cold and dark is all I see
    I'll find my rest by my Savior's side

By my dear Savior's side
His gift to me when He died
When He came from that tomb
He rescued me from my doom
When He rose that ascension day
To prepare me a place to stay
There forever I will abide
By my dear Savior's side

No fear or hurt will last for long
    My Lord will make me strong
    I'll find my strength by my Savior's side
Though crushed by man or land
Through my Lord I'll make my stand
    I'm always there by my Savior's side
Cunning tales charge all around
    I'll keep my feet on holy ground
    I'll find my goal by my Savior's side
The truth is here for all to see
    It was finished on Calvary's tree
    I'll find His grace by my Savior's side.   12-21-1995

THE DARK GLASS

For now a dark glass we see through
Not all His plans are we able to view
Soon no dark glass for any will be
But the perfect replacing mortality
For now I will pray and try to grow
Then and then on I will perfectly know
When I'm changed and an heir I'll be
I will be a son throughout all eternity
For now I will tend my given chore
I will strive to serve my holy Lord
But soon in a twinkling of an eye
My Lord will split the eastern sky

2-1992

MORTAL TRAVAIL

My Lord my straits are dire
I reside in this mud and mire
Cover me with grace from above
Give me your Fatherly love
Lift me up from mortal travail
I know through You I can prevail
My Lord at times I am unsure
I know that You are my only cure
With Your power, I will walk
Through Your Spirit, I will talk
You are my Lord and my God
Only You, my Lord do I laud.

11-1992

HEARING THE RAIN

I am hearing the rain
Dropping a drop and torrent at times
I have felt the cleansing
I have cherished the world's rhyme
The rain proves so much of You
Your plan, your grace, your love
Someday I will know and see
The product of your gracious love.   7-7-2015

LET ME

When I am laid to rest
I wish to have given my best
His grace will see me through
Let me to His cause be true
I've never loved enough or cared
I never given enough or shared
Time doesn't loom very long
In these last hours make me strong
Let me honor You on praying knees
Let me praise You for you saved me
Help me lead others to see
Give a servant's heart to me   4-1994

THAT RUGGED CROSS

In a beat of time, the time just a moment
He finished all for which He was sent
The King for me let a sinner repent
All my burdens through Him to relent

The tree means so much to a sinner like me
For He died the death on that old rugged tree

Thank God, thank God for that old rugged tree
He died on for you and me
My curse of sin no more must be
Thank God, thank God for that old rugged tree

Some may laugh and call it a joke
But for me He bore all my sin's yoke
He loved me so He died for me
In a beat of time on that rugged tree

No other could ever do what only Christ could do
He's the only one faithful and true, glory and Hallelu

Michele Whaley and David E. Clarke, 5-1995

WORK TO DO

All who have need
Hear His calling heed
Come join His crowd
He is Lord to all around
Do His work, serve long
Help His mission be strong
Help carry His cross
Tell the gospel to the lost
He died for all and for me
He died that we find relief
Believe, confess, come along
Witness so others belong

11-1992

LIFE'S FALLS

Life's falls descend over me
I am under the flow of it
Burdens rise as my confusion
But here in its middle I sit
My pain the more and more
Only one answer twas clear
Master heal my broken core
Jesus control and my life steer
I will praise you Lord of Lords
I will give all I have and all I say
Glory to the Father and His Son
Glory to the Spirit; for You I pray

3-1992

RISE, RISE

You sit and wait for an unknown source
      To help you in this desperate hour
Why don't you take up Jesus' course
      And feel His redeeming power

You feel, you've seen sorrow's way
      For life seems hard and lonely
Why don't you take time to pray
      To Christ upon bended knee

Now is the time to fix your goal
      Seize the cross's prize
Why don't you think of your soul
      See life through saved eyes

rise, rise
      and see the Lord
rise, rise see His majesty
      rise, rise, now is the time

walk with Him upon life's sea
      walk with Him upon life's sea

          Michele Whaley and David E. Clarke, 4-1995

A SPIRAL STAIRCASE

Refusing to answer the call
A spiral staircase we stride
Downward is our walk
Due to thoughts of self-pride
Right must be right
He is our divine might.   7-1-2000

AN EMOTIONAL SCAR

You say I must not cause in anyway
Any type or sort of emotional scar
But you rip our very soul away
And you cause us much harm
Life must be life, the road we choose
You take our soul due to ease
And throw it into a trash can
You ask where is the peace
Without a soul, one has a mean land
Life must be life, our all to lose.   7-1-2000

HIS GRACE

His grace allowed Himself to be
His grace caused the blind to see
His grace was cause for the tree
His grace saved a sinner like me

It's grace that lets me stand tall
It's grace that is my all
It's grace that was given to me
His grace let this blind man see

His love through grace to me was meant
His love in grace the veil was rent
His love through grace my sins repent
His love was why His grace was sent

I don't know why He sent His grace
Grace to walk this mortal pace
Then to go to His heavenly place
It's grace to me, His grace

Michele Whaley and David E. Clarke, 4-1995

SING

Sing my friends
> Sing your song

Sing if His grace
> Makes you strong

Sing my friends
> Sing with your all

Sing with song
> Stand so tall

For He's divine
> And a king

Through His grace
> We have everything

I sing with joy
> I sing with a shout

I sing to the One
> That life is all about

Sing my friends
> Sing your song

Sing if His grace
> Makes you strong

Sing my friends
> Sing with your all

Sing with song
> Stand so tall

For He's the Lord
> Gracious is He

He chose to save
> Both you and me

I sing with peace
> I sing to Him above

I sing to the One
> Who is divine love   4-20-1995

THE SON'S PSALM

I give You praise, my Lord of all
Compared to others, You stand tall
I give You glory, You are my King
You are my Savior, my everything
A remnant remains, I believe I'm one
I have belief; I confess you're the Son
This truth will win in the end
Victory over evil, victory over sin

In valleys and hills and desert land
You will lead, in you refuge I'll stand
You overshadow the truths of men
All of men's babble you transcend

My Lord, you will reign forever more
You through love knock on all doors
Your kingdom come, Father's free gift
Forever through You, I can live

11-1992

IN THE VALLEY

In the valley
Drawing close to Him
In the trying times
He purges my sin
In the valley
I need Him the more
He carries me o'er the hill
To His peaceful shore
Don't worry Christians
His light glows around
And in only a moment
You'll hear His sound
"Come from that land
Come up high to Me"
The Lord helps you stand
Someday His glory you'll see   4-1995

I STAND

I stand before the throne of God
With awe and fear I stand there
But by his grace and my faith
I am welcomed with love and care
I stand before the throne of God
He says welcome and come on in
I can rest and find His peace
Away from this life's failure and sin.   10-1996

AFTER THE STORM

In this deep valley,
Where fear grows large
I feel His calm breeze
His peace, His peace
Calms my heart
In His valley, I find relief

My Master, my Lord
My Savior, my King
My all in all
My everything
Storms come
Clouds so dark
My Master, my Lord
Steels my hearts

After the storm
Clouds roll back
I hear my heart say
His peace, His peace
Alieve the attack
I'll have a new day

In a day
Not long from here
I'll feel life slip away
His peace, His peace w
Will dry the tear
I'll be perfect on that day

7-16-2001

O HOLY GOD

O holy God
Thou hast brought me through the wilderness
Thou hast seen me through times of less
O holy God

My Lord, my Lord
How great Thou art
My Lord, my Lord
Live within my heart
O holy God, O holy God

O holy God
Thou hast covered me through the mountain high
Thou hast nurtured me through the valley cry
O holy God

My Lord, my Lord
How great Thou art
My Lord, my Lord
Live within my heart
O holy God, O holy God.   8-22-1999

THE ONE

The One who formed the all and all
        The One who created everything
The One who saved even me
        The One who is my eternal King.   10, 1996

NO EARTHLY GOOD

No cares of tomorrow
Where others have stood
I'm so full of heaven
I'm no earthly good
This old house
Not my neighborhood
I'm so full of heaven
I'm no earthly good
I'm no earthly good
As others may say
I live for the forever
Not the day to day
I see His cross
Not any mortal care
His hope I will share
My hope is Him
Pain and hurt
Always seem to be
This painful place
No home to me
I look to the sky
He'll brush away my tear
I'm so full of heaven
My home is not here
When I stand
In His glorious day
I'll have one thought
This I'll always pray
My goals are His
I'll do what I should
I'm so full of heaven
I'm no earthly good.   8-1995

THE LIGHT

In the dark and still of late night
I cherish His heaven sent light
When I do wrong and seldom do right
I know I have seen His redeeming light
His Spirit indwells me with His might
My God has sent me His saving light.   11-1992

LET ME PRAISE THE LORD

When rains fall on my mortal frame
        Let me praise the Lord
When I am weak and reveal my shame
        Let me praise the Lord
When life's struggle overcome me
        Let me raise His banner high
When I am vain, the Lord I need to see
        Let me raise His banner high
I am frail, but He reigns over all
        Be my Lord forever
I am weak, but He urges through my stall
        Be my Lord forever

I know to Him no one can compare
        Praises to my glorious God
I am rescued from every sin's snare
        Praises to my glorious God.   3-1992

TO SING TO YOU

Forever I lift up your name
You are most worthy to laud
If just for me, you would have came
You are the Son of God
To sing to you is a joyous thing
You are worthy my Lord
I sing of your righteous sword
You gave to me your hand
Through love you brought me high
Through you grace I can stand
Your precious love brings me nigh
I must sing and give praise
Though unworthy to do this
I tell of your gift all my days
Your plan finished, nothing amiss.

2-1992

BY MY SAVIOR'S SIDE

When I'm lost with nowhere to go
I'll cry out to one I know
I'll find my home by my Savior's side
Sudden night's all around me
Cold and dark is all I see
I'll find my rest by my Savior's side

By my Savior's side
　　　His gift to me when He died
When He came from that tomb
　　　He rescued me from my doom
When He rose that ascension day
　　　To prepare me a place to stay
And there forever I'll abide
　　　By my Dear Savior's side

No fear or hurt will last for long
My Lord will make me strong
I'll find my strength by my savior's side
Though crushed by man or land
Through my Lord I'll make my stand
I'm always there by my Savior's side

Cunning tales charge all around
I'll keep my feet on holy ground
I'll find my goal by my Savior's side
The truth is here for all to see
It was finished on Calvary
I'll find His grace by my Savior's side.　　　12-21-1995

THAT RUGGED TREE

In a beat of time
The time just a moment
He finished all
For which He was sent
The King for me
Let a sinner repent
Allowing all my burdens
Through Him to relent
That tree means so much
To a sinner like me
For He died the death
On that old rugged tree
Thank God, thank God
　　　For that old rugged tree
He died on for you and me
　　　My curse of sin no more must be
Thank God, thank God
　　　For that old rugged tree
Some may laugh
Calling Him a joke
But for you and me
He bore our sin's yoke
He loved me so
He died for me
In a beat of time
On that rugged tree
No other could ever do
What my Christ could do
He's the only one
Faithfull and true.

Michele Whaley and David E. Clarke, 5-1995

I'M THANKFUL

So quickly again, so suddenly once more
Thanksgiving is at the door
A time with family and friends
A season of memories, with beginnings and ends
I have seen faith and pain
I have seen patience standing the strain
Some have left, some have come
Some walk in service to God's Son
I'm thankful for those who seem so soon gone
Helped me much, helped me be strong
Those who walked with me during the year
Sharing my life, some laughter and tears
I am thankful for my church, a gathering of love
Who carried my weakness with help from above
I'm thankful to my Lord, for my life about me
Another year of grace and allowing me to be.   11-1997

HE SAVED ME

Lost, lonely and insecure
In life's complete despair
I felt an external lure
God really cares
Once lost in a land of sin
I held His hands scarred for me
He bore me from the state I was in
His Spirit came so like Him I could be
Mercies granted, the gulf removed
Not by me, but by God's own Son
The word He gives, His righteous truth
The word of Him, the one and only one
The fall's mire no longer stains me
Honor and praise to His name
Only Him do I want to see
He saved me, I am not the same.   3-1992

UP THE ROAD

Up the road so long ago
To the hill the trek so slow
Went a man with a heavy load
The price He paid worth more than gold

Up the road He bore our pain
He made a way for our gain
His unjust death paid my way
Through His blood I now can pray

Up the road, such a selfless act of love
        Up the road, God's Son came from above
To suffer death so I could be free
        Up the road to an old old tree

Up the road it was done on that cross
So no one must suffer loss
This giving act, given to me
Done by Christ on a cursed tree

For you see He died for me
His love so true He died for you
He suffered death so we could be free
Up the road to an old old tree
Yes, up the road to an old old tree.

Michelle Whaley and David E. Clarke, 4-1995

ANACHRONISTIC RHYME

I walk so indecisively
I do not speak as I should
To think my Lord died for me
I reach, but not as far as I could
Grace overshadows my corruptibility
His plan embraces and covers me
I called on the Lord on bended knee
God's Son, Messiah someday to see
Not turned for public reports
He uses my small gifts still
I pray I not be found short
I wish to always be in His will
I hope the Lord will accept my work
And my endeavor during my mortal time
With my walk and telling others of Him
In mortal words of anachronistic rhyme.   3-1992

GLORY

Glory, glory, glory to His holy name
Glory, glory, glory to His holy name
I am changed, will never be the same
I can only give glory to His holy name   3-1996

LET ME FIRMLY STAND

Bless this hard time Lord I pray
      Thank you for giving me another day
In these valleys of life take my hand
      In your cause let me firmly stand
Hold fast to those I love so much
      Let them know only You can they trust
Let me be your minister and man
      In your truth let me firmly stand
Be gracious and cover me with grace
      Let me march to your drum and pace
Let me share to everyone your plan
      In your power let me firmly stand
When I fail as I often tend to do
      Let me hold on to you who is true
Let me share and give to all the land
      In your mercy let me firmly stand.   8-1-2004

THE CROSS

I saw a cross this sunny bright day
Its beauty was He was no longer there
He rose and enabled us to pray
He went to Father. His gift to share
Draped about the cross a thorny crown
At the joint where the beams did meet
To show His love both up and around
He is Lord for the whole world to see
Also a purple robe hanging on the wood
A King unjustly accused, a willing Lamb
Helping and letting me be all I should
Allowing and keeping me be all I can.   4-28-1996

I CLING ON

There are times when I fail, but I cling on
There are times when life assails, but I cling on
There are times when I'm most low, but I cling on
There are times when I move slow, but I cling on

I cling to my Lord
        He is all I should be
I cling to His word
        And pray his grace covers me
I cling to His cross
        He is my only way
I cling to His love
        Every night and every day

In dark valleys I reside, but I cling on
All around seems to have lied, but I cling on
And my wants take hold, but I cling on
All I am is ne'er too bold, but I cling on

Soon I'll see His face, till then I'll cling on
I'll live in His place, till then I'll cling on
These days I should do more still I'll cling on
For He is my Lord, to Him I'll cling on.   4-1995

MY HOME

Why like other should I care for money or a name
      Why would I refuse to share making larger my guilty shame
For you see I'm just passing through. I'll soon be going up to
      My home, my real home

My home isn't here. My home has to tear
My Home I'll soon see, my home beckons me
My home I long for, my home will open its door
My home, my real home

This place with four bare walls never gave comfort to me
      I'll leave when my Father calls. In Heaven I want to be
Don't worry this isn't my home. In glory I'll soon roam
      My home, my real home

I really just can't wait to see my sweet Lord
      And walk through Heaven's gate when time cuts my cord
Once I've entered there I'll see my royal home fair
      My home, my real home.
              2007

A LAND, A CITY, A HOME

I saw a land with a city so fair.
I saw a home, in a land with no care
I wanted to run, I longed to be there
In my home in a city in a land so fair

A land, a land, a land for me
      A land, a land so grand to see
I saw a land with my lord for all
      A land, a land without death's dark pall

I saw my family waving at me
Come o'er to the city and cross life's sea
Lay frailty down, rest trav'ling man
in your home in a city in God's caring land

I saw my Lord astride His throne
In that city in a land near my home
My Lord arose, He beckoned me there
In His home, in His city, in His land so fair

My Lord called me to come o'er there
My Lord in a city in a land with no care.   1-19-2002

CONSIDERING

I ponder at the fast approach of the end of things as I knew them. Truths and truth itself is discarded in the existential relativistic selfishness of the 'me.' I have wondered and I now believe in the eternity, a person will come to the inevitable conclusion that they, like Huxley only wanted themselves as both god and accomplishment. The dread of such a conclusion reached. To find that one's doom rest in their own decision to be their own and demonstrating indeed they have only been a deluded and selfish slave to the fallen. The dread of such a conclusion held.

-The Old Testament-[4]

Genesis, the book of beginnings
  begin your work in me O Lord
  permit me to live in your court
Exodus, the book of names
  write your name in my soul
  allow your light in me to grow
Numbers, the book of wanderings
  let me wander in your land
  renew me to be a holy man
Leviticus, the book of the called
  call me Lord and I will go
  teach me your path to know
Deuteronomy, the book of words
  write your word in my heart
  guide my quest from the start
Joshua, the book of a mighty leader
  teach me your holy word
  let that be what others have heard
Judges, the book of a time of shame
  keep me in my pathway
  fortify me O Lord I pray
Ruth, the book of love
  help me love as you loved me O Lord
  outfit me with your divine sword
First Samuel, the book of change
  mold me to reflect your grace
  permit me to live before your face

---

[4] The Old Testament poem was first published in, "Eclectic Essays." FWB Publishing. c. 2011.

Second Samuel, the book of David
  let me cling to you
  let me to be a servant true
First Kings, the book of Solomon
  let your wisdom encircle my state
  let your righteousness hedge my estate
Second Kings, the book of war
  make me strong
  I wish to your cause to belong
First Chronicles, the book of Judah
  make me of your regal line
  fill me with your Spirit divine
Second Chronicles, the book of judgment
  adopt me into your royal family
  craft a loyal slave of me
Ezra, the book of the return
  return me to your place sublime
  enable me to be more kind
Nehemiah, the book of the second return
  give your peace to me
  demonstrate it for others to see
Esther, the book of a queen's love
  let me care for everyone around
  let your clarion call sound
Job, the book of faith during trouble
  save me from the trouble of this life
  remove from me evil's strife
Psalms, the book of praise
  let me praise your name renown
  I will give you my worker's crown
Proverbs, the book of wisdom
  give me wisdom and love
  let me reflect you above

Ecclesiastes, the book of the preacher
anoint me your message to speak
I will always your presence seek
Song of Solomon, the book of the wife
make and keep me your bride
in your refuge, let me hide
Isaiah, the book of the evangelical prophet
let me be meek
never find me weak
Jeremiah, the book of the broken hearted prophet
break my heart and take my pride
never let me hear your chide
Lamentations, the book of the temple's fall
keep me from failing you
let me be faithful all the way through
Ezekiel, the book of the prophet of change
change me into your image
I want to view your holy visage
Daniel, the book of the prophet of visions
give me a vision of your way
I will trust you all my days
Hosea, the book of the prophet to Israel
let me be faithful and wise
let me to see through your eyes
Joel, the book of the prophet to Judah
let me be receptive
let me your life live
Amos, the book of the prophet of judgment
judge me in my servant's lot
remove from me any evil plot

Obadiah, the book of the prophet to Edom
     judge me loyal
     my King so royal
Jonah, the book of the first prophet to Nineveh
     grant me mercy in your judgment
     in your service, make me adamant
Micah, the book of the prophet to the south
     grant me purity
     please Lord use me
Nahum, the book of the second prophet to Nineveh
     keep me from wrath
     set me on your straight path
Habakkuk, the book of the prophet who questioned
     let me bow on my knee
     only you do I want to see
Zephaniah, the book of the prophet of your coming
     keep me in your day
     keep me on your way
Haggai, the book of the prophet of the rebuilding
     make me serve
     enable me to never swerve
Zechariah, the book of the prophet of encouragement
     in all my ways and in all my days
     let me always your name praise
Malachi, the book of the prophet without compromise
     finish your work in me O Lord
     strengthen me to abide in your court   5-16-01

-THE NEW TESTAMENT-

Matthew, the book of the King
    My King and my Lord
    The Messiah of Israel's accord
Mark, the book of the Servant
    Let me serve and give
    Through You I may live
Luke, the book of the Son of Man
    You came as the One
    The serving obedient Son
John, the book of the Son of God
    Forever was, will and is
    Your plan with nothing amiss
The Acts of the Apostles, the book of transitions
    The growth and the plan
    Lord's remedy to fallen man
Romans, the book of the grace of the Lord
    From the worst to the best
    A plan to reveal and to attest
First Corinthians, the book of correction
    So many apart and away
    Let me come and not stray
Second Corinthians, the book of Paul's authority
    Paul, called to lead and sow
    The gentile bride to grow
Galatians, the book of our freedom
    Leave the law and be free
    His grace, the price of liberty
Ephesians, the book of our heavenly call
    Gracious Lord my all in all
    Precious Lord guide me to stand tall

Philippians, the book of our exhortation in holiness
  Set me apart and keep me strong
  Help me not err or go wrong
Colossians, the book of the preeminence of the Christ
  No one could be before
  No one, but You divine Lord
First Thessalonians, the book of correction and sanctification
  Hold to gracious truth and stay
  Hold fast against the tribulational sway
Second Thessalonians, the book of correction and comfort
  Let me grow during the strife
  Let me wait for You during this life
First Timothy, the book to be a faithful minister
  Let me stay the course and stand
  Watch over me and your given band
Second Timothy, the book to continue on
  Teach me and let me do the work
  Times are nearing which will hurt
Titus, the book of encouragement for strength
  Allow me to persevere against the falsity
  Permit me to work and stand and be
Philemon, the book of a slave and a master
  The master may be
  The slave is surely free
Hebrews, the book that Christ is better and best
  You are Lord above angels, fathers and law
  You are Lord first, last and above all
James, the book to the twelve tribes
  Strengthen me to be ready for the day
  Encourage me to work and never stray
First Peter, the book to bear our suffering
  My hope to be holy during the hard kind
  Suffering comes before the Lord's return time

Second Peter, the book contrasting truth and falsehood
      Let me rest in Your truth and not deny
      Let me beware of the evil apostate lie
First John, the book of fellowship
      Grant me to walk and obey Your love
      Pure and triumph through You, the Son
Second John, the book of pure steadfastness
      Always in the truth of You
      Shunning the lie always to be true
Third John, the book contrasting real and error
      Be true in godly generosity from the start
      Condemn the prideful and sinful heart
Jude, the book to guard against heresy
      Fallacy past, now and then
      Avoid the lie and the sin
The Revelation of Jesus Christ by John, the book of the finish
      The seventieth week soon will come
      The kingdom and bride of You, the glorious Son   07-2011